Excel Programming with VBA Starter

Get started with programming in Excel using Visual Basic for Applications (VBA)

Robert Martin

BIRMINGHAM - MUMBAI

Excel Programming with VBA Starter

Copyright © 2012 Packt Publishing

All rights reserved. No part of this book may be reproduced, stored in a retrieval system, or transmitted in any form or by any means, without the prior written permission of the publisher, except in the case of brief quotations embedded in critical articles or reviews.

Every effort has been made in the preparation of this book to ensure the accuracy of the information presented. However, the information contained in this book is sold without warranty, either express or implied. Neither the author, nor Packt Publishing, and its dealers and distributors will be held liable for any damages caused or alleged to be caused directly or indirectly by this book.

Packt Publishing has endeavored to provide trademark information about all of the companies and products mentioned in this book by the appropriate use of capitals. However, Packt Publishing cannot guarantee the accuracy of this information.

First published: October 2012

Production Reference: 1171012

Published by Packt Publishing Ltd.
Livery Place
35 Livery Street
Birmingham B3 2PB, UK.

ISBN 978-1-84968-844-4

www.packtpub.com

Credits

Author
Robert Martin

Reviewers
Jan Karel Pieterse
Peter M Taylor

Acquisition Editor
Alex Newbury

Commissioning Editor
Meeta Rajani

Technical Editor
Vrinda Amberkar

Project Coordinator
Shraddha Bagadia

Proofreader
Aaron Nash

Indexer
Hemangini Bari

Production Coordinator
Prachali Bhiwandkar

Cover Work
Prachali Bhiwandkar

Cover Image
Conidon Miranda

www.PacktPub.com

Support files, eBooks, discount offers and more

You might want to visit `www.PacktPub.com` for support files and downloads related to your book.

Did you know that Packt offers eBook versions of every book published, with PDF and ePub files available? You can upgrade to the eBook version at `www.PacktPub.com` and as a print book customer, you are entitled to a discount on the eBook copy. Get in touch with us at `service@packtpub.com` for more details.

At `www.PacktPub.com`, you can also read a collection of free technical articles, sign up for a range of free newsletters and receive exclusive discounts and offers on Packt books and eBooks.

www.PacktLib.PacktPub.com

Do you need instant solutions to your IT questions? PacktLib is Packt's online digital book library. Here, you can access, read and search across Packt's entire library of books.

Why Subscribe?

- Fully searchable across every book published by Packt
- Copy and paste, print and bookmark content
- On demand and accessible via web browser

Free Access for Packt account holders

If you have an account with Packt at www.PacktPub.com, you can use this to access PacktLib today and view nine entirely free books. Simply use your login credentials for immediate access.

Table of Contents

Excel Programming with VBA Starter — 1
So, what is VBA? — 3
- The basic features of VBA — 3
- What kind of things can you do with it? — 3
- How can you use this technology within your existing projects? — 3

Recording a macro, adding modules, browsing objects, and variables — 4
- Recording a macro — 4
  - Option 1 – Recording a macro from the status bar — 4
  - Option 2 – Recording from the Developer tab — 4
- Executing your code — 6
- Saving a workbook containing macros — 7
- Adding a module — 8
- Browsing objects — 8
- Working with variables — 9
- The Immediate window — 11
- And that's it — 12

Quick start – VBA programming — 13
- Working with loops — 13
  - Method 1 – For-Next loops — 13
  - Method 2 – For Each-Next Loops — 15
  - Method 3 – Do-While and Do-Until loops — 17
- Dimensioning and instantiating objects — 20
- Subroutines and user-defined functions — 23
  - Subroutines — 23
  - Functions — 24

Table of Contents

Top features you'll want to know about	**31**
Enumeration	31
Classes	32
External libraries	40
People and places you should get to know	**44**
Official sites	44
Resources	44
Articles and tutorials	44
Community	44
Blogs	44
Twitter	45
Index	**47**

Excel Programming with VBA Starter

Welcome to Excel VBA Starter. This book has been especially created to provide you with all the information that you need to get up to speed with programming with VBA (Visual Basic for Applications). You will learn the basics of VBA, get started with building your first VBA code, create user-defined functions to work out complex calculations, and see the tricks of the trade when it comes to using VBA with Excel.

This document contains the following sections:

So what is VBA? – find out what VBA actually is, what you can do with it, and why it's so great.

Recording a macro, adding modules, browsing objects, and variables – learn how to record a macro, add modules, browse for objects available in your project, and finally what variables are useful for.

Quick start: VBA programming – this section will get you started on programming with VBA. Here you will learn how to perform some core tasks in VBA. Such tasks include using loops, dimensioning objects, and creating and categorizing **User-defined Functions (UDFs)**.

Top features you need to know about – VBA gives you infinite possibilities when it comes to creating your own solutions. In this section, you will learn some key concepts such as enumeration, classes (defining properties and methods), and referencing external libraries, in particular how to manipulate files and folders.

People and places you should get to know – in this day and age, it is impossible to live without the Internet and it is here that you can find resources as well as help for your VBA woes. This section provides you with many useful links to the project page and forums, as well as a number of helpful articles, tutorials, blogs, and the Twitter feeds of VBA super-contributors.

So, what is VBA?

In this section, you will get to know a bit about VBA, its basic features, what you can do with it, and how you can put it to work with a view to facilitating your daily work, by automating common tasks.

The basic features of VBA

Visual Basic for Applications (**VBA**) is a programming language built into Microsoft Office applications. As you improve your skills in any application from the Office System, you will eventually realize that although Microsoft Office applications offer a large number of tools, they do not offer everything you need to perform your daily chores. Such chores may include creating a corporate custom-format, a custom function that calculates commission payments, and so on.

Thus, VBA works as a gap-filler; in other words, its main purpose is to ensure that you can do whatever you need to do in your job.

What kind of things can you do with it?

Once you have pushed your experience using the Office application to the limits and you can no longer get your job done due to a lack of built-in tools, using VBA will help avert frustrations you may encounter along the way. VBA enables you to build custom functions, also called **User-defined Functions** (**UDFs**), and you can automate tedious tasks such as defining and cleaning formats, manipulate system objects such as files and folders, as well as work together with Windows as a combined system, through its **Application Programming Interface** (**API**), and other applications by referencing their object libraries or **Dynamic-link Libraries** (**DLLs**).

Of course you can also use VBA to manipulate the Office application that hosts your code. For example, you can customize the user interface in order to facilitate the work you and others do.

An important thing to remember, though, is that the VBA code that you create is used within the host application. In our case, the code will run within Excel. Such VBA programs are not standalone, that is, they cannot run by themselves; they need the host application in order to operate correctly.

How can you use this technology within your existing projects?

You can use VBA in two different ways. The first, and most common way is to code directly into your VBA project. For example, you may have an Excel workbook with some custom functions that calculate commissions. You can add modules to this workbook and code the UDFs in this module.

Another option would be to save the workbook as an **Addin**. An Addin is a specialized document that hosts the code and makes it available to other workbooks. This is very useful when you need to share the solutions you develop with other workbooks and co-workers.

Excel Programming with VBA Starter

Recording a macro, adding modules, browsing objects, and variables

Before you get your hands "dirty" with coding in VBA, there are a few things you need to know. These things will help when it comes to coding. In this section, you will learn how to:

- Record a macro
- Add modules
- Browse objects
- Get some background on declaring variables

We will start with macro recording, a feature which is available in most Office applications.

Recording a macro

A **macro**, in Office applications, is a synonym for VBA code. In Excel, we can record almost any action we perform (such as mouse clicks and typing), which in turn is registered as VBA code. This can come in handy when we need to discover properties and methods related to an object. Let us now have a look at some ways you can record a macro in Excel. There are two options:

1. Recording a macro from the status bar.
2. Recording from the **Developer** tab.

Option 1 – Recording a macro from the status bar

From the status bar, click on the **Record Macro** button. If the button is not visible, right-click on the status bar and from the pop-up menu, choose the **Macro Recording** option, as shown in the following screenshot:

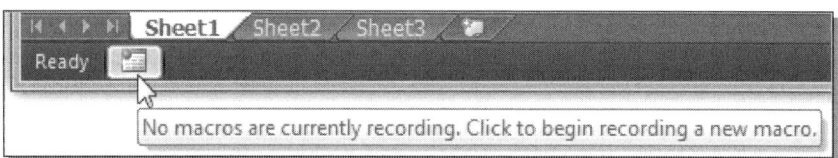

Option 2 – Recording from the Developer tab

Now that you know how to record a macro from the status bar, let us check another option. This option requires that you activate the **Developer** tab. In order to activate it, assuming it is not active yet, follow these steps:

1. Go to **File | Excel Options | Customize Ribbon**.

2. Under **Main Tabs** check the **Developer** checkbox, as shown in the following screenshot:

3. Next, activate the **Developer** tab and click on **Record Macro**, as shown in the following screenshot:

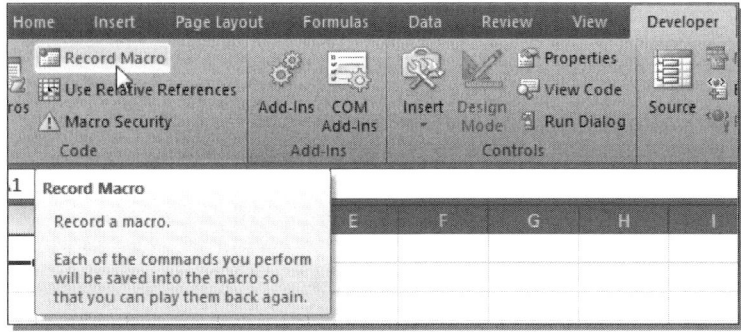

4. Once the macro recording process starts, you will be prompted to enter some basic information about the macro such as the macro name, the shortcut key, location where the macro should be stored, and its description. The following screenshot shows these options filled out:

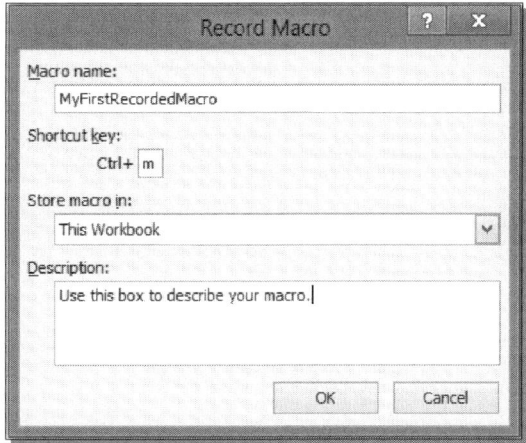

5. Once the macro has been recorded, you can access its container module by pressing, simultaneously, the *Alt + F11* keys. Alternatively, you can click on the **Visual Basic** button in the **Developer** tab. This button is to the left of the **Record Macro** button introduced previously. This will open the **Visual Basic Editor** (**VBE**), where all the VBA code is kept.

The VBE is the tool we use to create, modify, and maintain any code we write or record. The following screenshot shows the VBE window with the project explorer, properties, and code window visible:

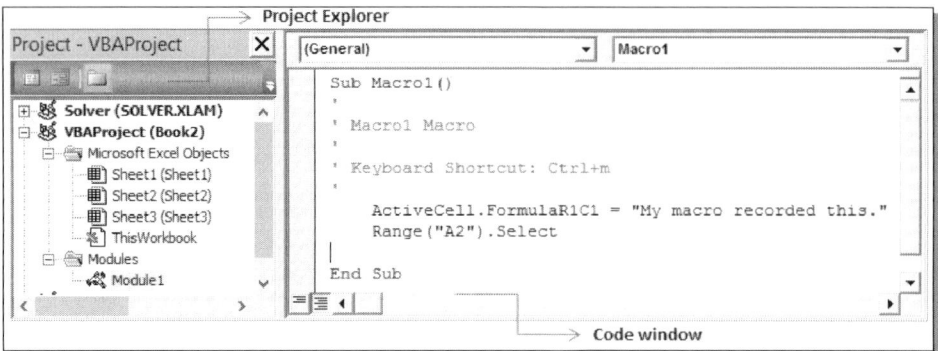

6. If upon opening the VBE, the VBA project explorer window is not visible, then follow these steps:

    1. Go to **View | Project Explorer.**
    2. Alternatively, press the *Ctrl + R* keys simultaneously.

7. If, on the other hand, the VBA project explorer is visible, but the code window is not, you can choose which code window to show.

8. Suppose you are interested in the content of the module you've recorded from the project explorer window, follow these step to show the module window:

    1. Click on **View | Code.**
    2. Alternatively, press F7.

Executing your code

Once you have recorded your macro, if you have added a shortcut to it, then you will be able to run the code by using this keyboard combination.

However, if you are coding directly into the container object (a user form, standard module, class module, and so on), then you may have to use different methods in case there is no shortcut to your procedures.

Here are some methods you can use to execute your code (all of them assume you have the Visual Basic Editor open):

- **Pressing the function key F5**: Place the cursor inside the procedure you wish to execute and press the function key **F5**. This will run your entire procedure.

- **Pressing the function key F8**: When you press the function key *F8*, you will step into your code. This means that each line will be executed only when you press this key. This is a great method if you need to check line by line within your code or a section of your code.
- **Pressing the Ctrl + F8 keys simultaneously**: This will force the code run until it finds the mouse cursors placed in your code. The cursor is the blinking beam that represents your mouse pointer.
- **Call the code from the Immediate window**: See the *Immediate window* section in this guide for instructions on how this is done.
- **Click on the "play" button**: On the standard toolbar, click on the "play" button. This has the same effect as pressing the function key *F5*. If the toolbar is not visible, go to **View | Toolbars | Standard**.

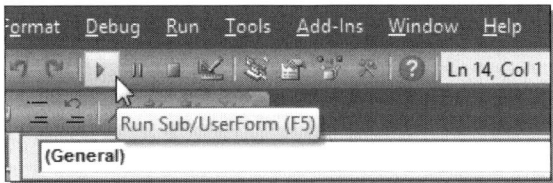

Saving a workbook containing macros

Before you get too excited with coding in VBA, be aware that Excel has specific file formats which are appropriate for specific tasks. The default file format does not allow you to save embedded macros in it. This format ends with the extension .xlsx. Any macros placed in such a file will be wiped out.

When it is time to save your Excel workbook, you must select the **Excel Macro-Enabled Workbook (*.xlsm)** type (which ends with the extension xlsm). The open format (xlsm) is the preferred format. However, you can also use the binary format (xlsb) or, to ensure the code can be run in older versions of Excel, you can use the xls format:

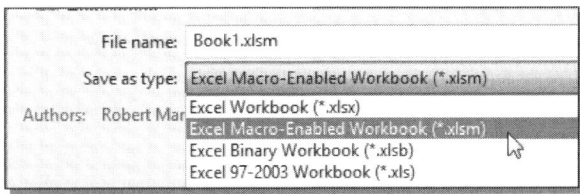

You can easily distinguish the files by their desktop icons. The macro-enabled workbook has an exclamation mark, while the macro-free version does not.

Adding a module

You add code to the code window of any object. These objects can be the workbook itself (also called **ThisWorkbook**; see the screenshot in the *Immediate window* section), the worksheet object, user forms, modules, and class modules. Your choice will depend on the usage of the code. If the code needs to be public, then you should add it to a module.

In order to add a module, follow these steps:

1. Go to **Insert | Module**.
2. Alternatively, right-click anywhere in the **Project Explorer** window and from the pop-up menu, go to **Insert | Module**.

Browsing objects

The **Object Browser** is a very important tool that you can use to check for the properties and methods of an object as well as any other information related to that object.

In order to access the Object Browser, follow these steps:

1. Go to **View | Object Explorer**.
2. Alternatively, press the function key *F2* on your keyboard.

Once the Object Browser is open, you will be presented with the window shown in the following screenshot. From the first drop-down list you can choose which library you want to browse to. You can browse all libraries in one go or you can browse a specific library. In the following example, the active library is **Excel**. Below it, there is a list with all the classes (objects) available in the Excel object library. Currently, the active class is **Range** and to its right you have all the properties and methods that are members of this class:

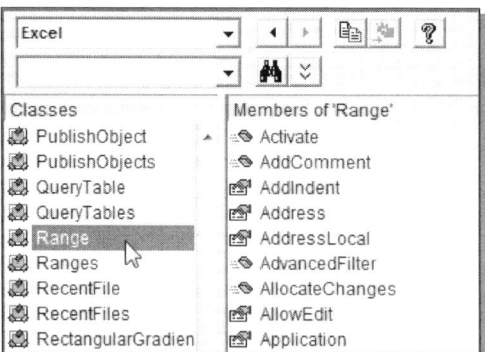

The methods are represented by a small "running brick" whereas the properties are represented by a hand holding a card.

Methods are named using verbs while properties are named using nouns. Methods represent procedures, that is, actions to be performed or functions. Therefore, the Activate method is a procedure that activates the object Range, which has been specified in the code. Similarly, properties refer to the qualities of the object. For example, the Name property can be used to retrieve the name of a worksheet as well as to rename it. Properties can be read-only, write-only, or read-write.

If you find that confusing, you can think of it in terms of your own body. For example, Height is a property that tells how tall you are, whereas Grow is a method (think of this method as a growth hormone) that instructs your body to grow.

Finally, you can search for properties and methods while in this window. Simply enter what you are looking for in the box right under the Excel box, as shown in the following screenshot. The Object Browser will show you all the matching results with the corresponding class and its membership:

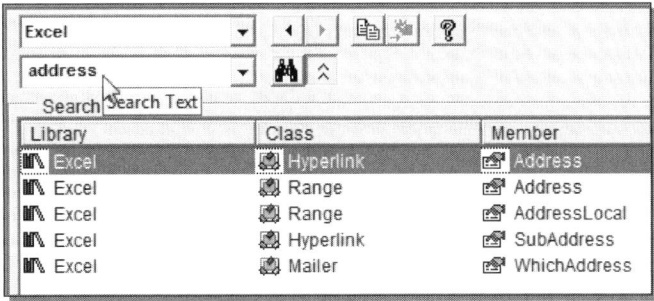

Working with variables

One important aspect of VBA programming lies in declaring your variables. **Variables**, as the name suggests, are things that vary or change over a period of time. Therefore, a variable could be specific such as a text string, a number (such as integer and long), or an object. But it can also be a variant, which means it takes no specific shape to begin with, but it will take whatever shape it is set to later on in your code.

It is not a prerequisite that you declare your variables (unless the container has the key phrase Option Explicit placed on the first line of the code window). In this scenario we have what we call **implicit declaration**, that is, you don't declare any variables and let VBA automatically create a variant type whenever a variable is needed.

Forcing explicit variable declaration is a good practice as it improves code performance, it makes reading your code easier (for others and yourself), and it also avoids ambiguity in your code. If you want the compiler to force variable declarations, follow these steps to switch on explicit variable declaration:

1. Open the Visual Basic Editor.

2. Go to **Tools | Options**.
3. When the **Options** dialog box open, activate the **Editor** tab (if it is not active), and check the **Require Variable Declaration** option.

Variables can be declared as:

- `Private`: A private variable implies that it can only be accessed by its container object. In other words, if a variable is declared as private inside a module, it is only accessible by the module that contains it. By default, declarations inside built-in objects (user forms, `ThisWorkbook`, worksheets, and classes) are private. Declaring a variable as public within such objects only changes the scope at the object level, not at the project level.

- `Public`: A public variable implies that any object within your project can access it, as long as it is declared in a standard module. Public variables must be placed inside standard modules if you want their scope to be global (project level).

The preceding declarations relate to accessibility of the variables you declare. However, there are other keywords you can use in the declaration:

- `Dim`: This stands for Dimension and is the most common way to declare a variable
- `Static`: This determines that the variable must remain static throughout the execution of your code
- `Const`: This determines that the variable must remain constant throughout the execution of your code

The following code snippet illustrates the usage of such declarations and combinations. Explanations are embedded in the code:

```
'Variable which is only accessible within this module
Private myInteger          As Integer

'Variable accessible from anywhere within this VBA Project
Public myExcelRange        As Excel.Range

'Constant accessible from anywhere within this VBA Project
Public Const myString      As String = "This text will not change."

'Declaring variables within a producedure
Sub DeclaringVariables()
'   Static variable will retain its previously
'   assigned value across the same session
    Static MyStaticCounter  As Long

'   Early binding of an object
    Dim myAppExcel          As Excel.Application
End Sub
```

The Immediate window

The **Immediate** window allows you to display information related to the debugging of your code. **Debugging** refers to the process of finding and mitigating "bugs". **Bugs** are coding mistakes that cause your program to deviate from its original intended use. The Immediate window will also execute commands that you type directly into it. It appears, by default, at the bottom of Visual Basic Editor (VBE) window:

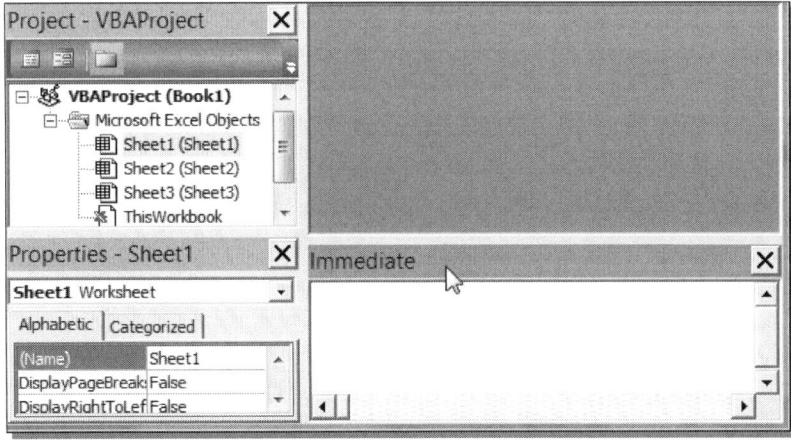

To display the **Immediate** window (if it is not active), follow these steps:

1. Go to **View | Immediate window**.
2. Alternatively, press *Ctrl + G* simultaneously (press *F7* to jump back to the code window).

The **Immediate** window has many uses, some of which we will look at now. To demonstrate the possibilities, ensure that the **Immediate** window is active and replicate the following code snippets in a standard module; then, execute it:

- **Debugging problems in your code**: This first method uses debug.print and it is great if you need to find out what is going on in your code. A code sample as follows. Copy it into a standard module and execute it.

    ```
    Sub ErrorCode()
        On Error Resume Next
        MyRandomNumber = Rnd() / 0
        Debug.Print Err.Description
    End Sub
    ```

    In this example, we instruct VBA to resume the next line of code if it finds an error. As division by zero is not defined, an error will occur. Then, we use the `Print` method of the `Debug` object to write the description of the error to the **Immediate** window.

+ **Calling a procedure or function**: Using the same example code just used, on the **Immediate** window, write the following and then press *Enter*:

    ```
    Call ErrorCode()
    ```

    This will force the execution of the procedure entitled `ErrorCode()`. As the procedure generates an error, the error description will also be written to the **Immediate** window.

    If you are calling a function, however, you will need to do something slightly different. As an example, copy the following function into a standard module:

    ```
    Function MyNameIs() As String
        MyNameIs = "Robert Friedrick Martin"
    End Function
    ```

    The function simply returns my name. It has no other use, but supposing this was an internal function and you wanted to know my name, you could call this function from the **Immediate window** as follows:

    ```
    ?MyNameIs
    ```

    Upon execution, the output will be shown in the **Immediate** window, as shown in the following screenshot (previous example included):

    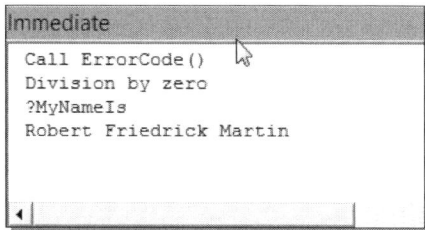

+ **Executing the code**: You can run code straight from the **Immediate** window. Let us take the first example given in this section. Let us suppose we want to check what happens to the division before putting that line of code in your procedure. We can run the following in the **Immediate** window (press *Enter* after entering the procedure):

    ```
    MyRandomNumber = Rnd() / 0
    ```

And that's it

In this section, you have learned some basic stuff about VBA. These included macro recording, adding modules, and browsing objects.

You also learned how to use the immediate window to debug your code. This feature is very important because it allows you to carry out many critical debugging tests.

With these tools mastered, you are now able to move on to the next step of your VBA quest.

Quick start – VBA programming

Now that you have the basic understanding about VBA (recording a macro, adding modules, browsing objects, and declaring variables), it is time to get to work.

In this section you will learn how to:

- Use loops
- Dimension and instantiate objects
- Create sub routines and user-defined functions

Working with loops

You will start your programming trip down the VBA lane by learning a bit about loops. Loops allow you to repeat a set of instuctions until a predetermined condition changes or a criterion is met.

Loops are extremely important, so you should study and practice this section carefully. You will now be introduced to different looping methods. We will start with For-Next loops.

Method 1 – For-Next loops

If you need to count something or you need to loop through a series of predetermined elements within a given set, then you should look no further. This is because once you specify the start and end values and the loop takes place, the counter starts to run. Suppose that the start value is 1 and the end value is 10 (all values being integers). Then, assuming the loop goes from beginning to end, the counter value will be 11 when the loop finishes to run its course. This is so because the counter is inclusive, that is, it must include the last value when the loop was called. On the other hand, suppose the loop exits at the Exit For statement; then the counter value will depend on the condition that forced the exit. Suppose the condition states that if the counter is equal to 5, then it must exit. The counter value at the exit point will equal to 5. However, if the set condition is greater than 5 at the first value greater than 5, the loop will exit. This value will be 6 (assuming we are dealing with integers). The basic syntax for this loop type is as follows:

```
For counter = start To end [Step step]
   [statements]
[Exit For]
   [statements]
Next [counter]
```

In the Next [counter] part, there is no need to specify the [counter] label. In spite of this, whether you happen to have many nested loops (loops inside loops) or not, it is a good idea to explicitly specify which counter you refer to. This is so because it is quite easy to get confused as the code grows in complexity.

It may sound redundant, but the variable can increase or decrease in value each time it moves to the next value.

Here's a simple example:

```
Sub ForNextLoopExample()
'   Dimensions (Declares) the "i" variable as an
'   integer type
    Dim i       As Integer

'   Dimensions (Declares) the "iCount" variable as an
'   integer type
    Dim iCount  As Integer

'   Loop from "i" equals 1 until
'   it reaches the value equal to 100:
    For i = 1 To 100
'       Add 1 to the counter value.
'       In order to keep the addition going
'       iCount is added to itself plus 1:
        iCount = iCount + 1
'   Move to the next "i" variable in the loop
'   Keep doing this until it reaches the value 100
    Next i

'   Display the counter in a message box
    MsgBox iCount
End Sub
```

Here, the loop runs from the integer 1 to 100 and adds 1 to the counter variable each time the loop moves to the next value. You should notice that the variable `iCount` is not needed. Thus, your code could look as follows (it will be 1 larger than the previous code as it goes from 1 to 100 inclusive):

```
Sub ForNextLoopExample2()
'   Dimensions the "i" variable as an
'   integer type
    Dim i       As Integer

'   Loop from "i" equals 1 until
'   it reaches the value equal to 100
    For i = 1 To 100
    Next i


'   Display the "i" variable in a message box
    MsgBox i
End Sub
```

By pressing *F8* successively you will be able to more clearly see how the code actually works. As you move through the code, stop, and point the mouse pointer to the variable so that you can inspect its value at that given point.

You can obtain the exact same effect as the preceding loop as follows:

```
Sub SteppedLoopExample()
    Dim i           As Double
    Dim iCounter    As Integer

'   Loop from 0 to 1 with a step
'   equivalent to one-hundredth of 1 (0.01)
    For i = 0 To 1 Step 0.01
        iCounter = iCounter + 1
    Next i
    MsgBox iCounter
End Sub
```

What was done in the preceding code is similar to dividing one pound into 100 pence (or £ 0.01). Therefore, between 0 and 1 there are a hundred units, which is the same as counting from 1 to 100, as we did in the first loop.

One detail here is that the data type had to be changed from Integer to Double for the i variable. This change is necessary because the step is not an integer. If we leave the i variable as an integer, we will get an infinite loop, as the loop will never manage to move from 0 (zero) to the next step, as 0.01 will be taken to be 0 (zero).

Method 2 – For Each-Next Loops

This kind of loop will repeat a block of statements for each object in a collection or each element in an array. For example, you could loop through each Worksheet (object) in the Sheets (collection). Given that you will move through a series of objects in a collection, VBA will automatically set the variable each time the loop runs.

The syntax for this loop type is as follows:

```
For Each element In group
   [statements]
[Exit For]
   [statements]
Next [element]
```

The next sample code reads through each file in the folder where the workbook is located. It then lists each file in the active worksheet.

Excel Programming with VBA Starter

For this example, you will be introduced to an interesting programming concept – **referencing**. In VBA we can reference external libraries so that we can benefit from their **Object Model** (**OM**). The OM, in this context, refers to the collection of objects that belong to such a library. Does that sound confusing? Then imagine a real library with a collection of books (objects). There are thousands of libraries across the world and if you become a member, you will have access to their collections of books. In the same fashion, if you reference the Microsoft Outlook Object Library, you will have access to all its objects.

Here, we have to add a reference to the Windows Script Hosting Model. In order to do so, you must follow these steps:

1. Open the Visual Basic Editor (VBE) window.
2. Go to **Tools | References**.
3. Once the dialog box is open, scroll down until you find the **Windows Script Hosting Model**. Once you find it, select it and close the dialog box.

```
Sub ListFilesInThisFolder()
'   Dimensions the File System object
    Dim oFSO            As New FileSystemObject

'   Dimensions the Folder object
    Dim oFSOFolder      As Folder

'   Dimensions the File object
    Dim oFSOFile        As File

'   Dimensions the row counter and
'   the string the will hold the path
'   for this workbook
    Dim lRowCount       As Long
    Dim sFilePath       As String

'   Sets the file path for this workbook
    sFilePath = ThisWorkbook.Path

'   Sets the folder, based on where this workbook
'   is located, in order to pick the files containing
'   in it.
    Set oFSOFolder = oFSO.GetFolder(sFilePath)

'   Sets the lower bound for the row counter
    lRowCount = 1

'   For each file in the folder
```

```
        For Each oFSOFile In oFSOFolder.Files
'           Get the file name and write it to the ActiveSheet
'           in the cell whose row number is equal to lRowCount
'           and column is equal to 1
            ActiveSheet.Cells(lRowCount, 1) = oFSOFile.Name

'           Add 1 to the row counter
            lRowCount = lRowCount + 1

'       Move to the next file found in the folder
        Next oFSOFile

'       Clean the objects from memory
        Set oFSOFile = Nothing
        Set oFSOFolder = Nothing
        Set oFSO = Nothing
    End Sub
```

Method 3 – Do-While and Do-Until loops

These two loop types will run while a condition is true or until the condition becomes true. The syntax for these two types of loops is as follows:

```
Do [{While | Until} condition]
[statements]
[Exit Do]
[statements]
Loop
```

In the preceding example, the condition was specified before entering the loop. However, these two methods also give the flexibility to determine the condition after the loop has started. For example:

```
Do
[statements]
[Exit Do]
[statements]
Loop [{While | Until} condition]
```

Unlike the For-Next loop mentioned in the previous section that executes until it reaches the last "next number" or object in the sequence, a Do While or Do Until must reach a true condition before it stops looping. This can obviously result in an infinite loop if a true value cannot be attained.

So, let us suppose you have a series of values in the first column of the active worksheet and you need to determine the address of the last empty cell. You could do so using the following code:

```
Sub DoUntilLoop()
'    Dimensions the row counter
     Dim lRowCounter As Long

'    Sets the lower bound of the row counter
     lRowCounter = 1

'    Run the loop until it finds the first empty cell
'    in the first column of the active sheet
     Do Until IsEmpty(ActiveSheet.Cells(lRowCounter, 1))
         lRowCounter = lRowCounter + 1
     Loop

'    When the first empty cell in column 1 is found,
'    display its address in a message box
     MsgBox ActiveSheet.Cells(lRowCounter, 1).Address
End Sub
```

Bear in mind that this code will return the first empty cell (see the following screenshot):

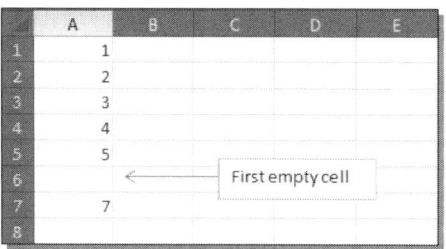

It does not mean that below this particular cell there is nothing else. If you really needed to determine the last cell with data, a better option would be as follows:

```
Sub GetLastRowAddress()
'    Display the address of the last non-empty row
'    in a message box. This is equivalente to pressing
'    CTRL + Up Arrow
     MsgBox ActiveSheet.Range("A1048000").End(xlUp).Address
End Sub
```

Downloading the example code

You can download the example code files for all Packt books you have purchased from your account at http://www.packtpub.com. If you purchased this book elsewhere, you can visit http://www.packtpub.com/support and register to have the files e-mailed directly to you.

The following example will be executed while the random number is smaller than 80. Once the condition is true, the loop exits and displays a message telling us the number found and how many times the loop was executed before exiting.

```
Sub DoWhileLoop()
    Dim iMyRandomInteger        As Integer
    Dim lLoopCounter            As Long

'   Randomize so that a new seed value is set;
'   for the Rnd() function
    Randomize
    iMyRandomInteger = Int((100 * Rnd) + 1)

'   Do the loop while the random number is
'   not greater than 80
    Do While (Not (iMyRandomInteger > 80))
        iMyRandomInteger = Int((100 * Rnd) + 1)
        lLoopCounter = lLoopCounter + 1
    Loop

'   Display a message box showing the random value that
'   caused the loop to exit. It also shows the number of
'   times that the loop ocurred before it exited.
    MsgBox "Loop exited... The exit value is equal to: " & _
        iMyRandomInteger & ". Loop was executed " & _
        lLoopCounter & " times before exiting.", vbInformation

End Sub
```

It is important to emphasize that if we omit the `Randomize` statement, the `Rnd` function will use the same number as a seed whenever it is called for the first time. This will give the impression that you are not getting a random number, which will be true if you are using the first number, and thereafter uses the last generated number as a seed value.

The While loop type can also end with the keyword `Wend`:

```
While
    [statements]
Wend
```

This loop construct does exactly the same thing as the previous example. The usage depends on the programmer and his/her preferences.

Dimensioning and instantiating objects

You already know how to dimension a variable. You basically add the keyword `Dim` before your variable and then define its type. When you studied the second looping method you were introduced to referencing libraries. However, nothing was said about the object used, to be exact, the `FileSystemObject`.

When we work with objects we can dimension them explicitly or implicitly by using either the true object or by using the generic class, namely, `Object`.

Here's how it looks explicitly:

```
Sub DimensioningAnObject()
    Dim objFSO        As FileSystemObject
End Sub
```

And generically, it will look like this:

```
Sub DimensioningAnObject()
    Dim objFSO        As Object
End Sub
```

It should be clear from the preceding code that the first method is preferred to the second, given that anyone reading your code would immediately identify what the object (`objFSO`) is. Notice that in the second example the object can be set to be any kind of object even though its dimension name may suggest something else. Therefore, you could set it to be the application object, if that was your desire.

However, it is important to point out that you can only dimension an object in this way (first example, just covered) if it belongs to the project. Objects that belong to the Excel application will always be available though. Other objects, such as `FileSystemObject`, must be referenced.

Whether you reference an object or you are using the default objects belonging to the application, this is known as **early binding**, that is, you bind (expose) the objects to the VBA project from the outset.

Therefore, `EarlyBinding` could look as follows (the explanation is embedded in the following code):

```
Sub EarlyBinding()
'   Dimension the object explicitly
    Dim objAppExcel    As Excel.Application

'   On error the code should resume the next line
'   This is because we are trying to "get" the
'   Excel Application Object, but it does not exist
'   an error will be thrown
    On Error Resume Next
```

```vba
        Set objAppExcel = GetObject(, "Excel.Application")

    '   If the objAppExcel is still nothing (it was not set
    '   in the previous line), then the object should be created
        If objAppExcel Is Nothing Then _
            Set objAppExcel = CreateObject("Excel.Application")

    '   Show the caption of window 1
        MsgBox objAppExcel.Windows(1).Caption

    '   Destroys the object
        Set objAppExcel = Nothing
    End Sub
```

Now, let us suppose you are developing a VBA application that will work with different versions of Excel. In this case, a **late binding** is more appropriate. Why? Because the generic object can take any shape and form. Therefore, it will not matter whether you are working with Excel 97, Excel 2010, or future releases. In fact, it does not matter for any object type, as Object is just an abstraction.

To make matters clearer, try to describe a bird. Most people would describe a feathery animal that sings and flies. However, a bird is an abstraction because not all birds sing or fly. Until you get down to the specifics, that is, set (define) which bird you are talking about, it could be a prehistoric bird for all anyone knows.

This is why late binding is great, as you do not need to specify what it is until it is really necessary.

The following example shows how late binding could be attained:

```vba
    Sub LateBinding()
    '   Dimension the object implicitly
        Dim objAppExcel     As Object

    '   On error the code should resume the next line
    '   This is because we are trying to "get" the
    '   Excel Application Object, but it does not exist
    '   an error will be thrown
        On Error Resume Next
        Set objAppExcel = GetObject(, "Excel.Application")

    '   If the objAppExcel is still nothing (it was not set
    '   in the previous line), then the object should be created
        If objAppExcel Is Nothing Then _
            Set objAppExcel = CreateObject("Excel.Application")

    '   Show the caption of window 1
```

```
            MsgBox objAppExcel.Windows(1).Caption

    '   Destroys the object
            Set objAppExcel = NothingEnd Sub
```

The code is basically the same presented previously, but the Excel application object is defined from the outset.

Another important point you should know about working with objects is that they need to be set. In the previous examples this is done at the following line of code:

```
            Set objAppExcel = GetObject(, "Excel.Application")
```

However, if you are using early binding, you can also set the object at the same time you dimension it:

```
            Dim objAppExcel       As New Excel.Application
```

Notice the keyword **New** just before the object. When an object is created like this, there is no need for you to set it.

 When you set an object using the preceding method, memory is allocated to handle calls to its library. In the preceding example, the Excel application starts to run in the background. You can view this by accessing the Task Manager. You can open the Task Manager by pressing the keys *Ctrl + Shift + Esc* simultaneously.

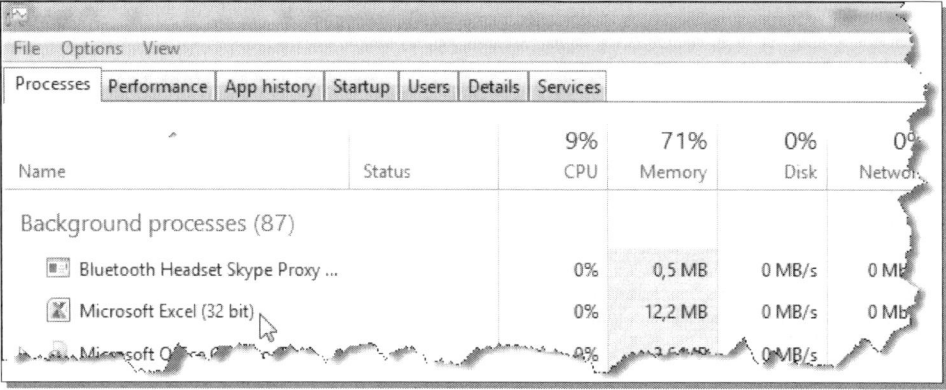

Subroutines and user-defined functions

In the previous topics, you were indirectly introduced to subroutines, but you were not taught their true meaning and function.

In this topic you will learn a bit about subroutines and user-defined functions specifically.

Subroutines

Routines, also known as procedures, are defined as a set of logical instructions (methods) that are used to regulate an activity or how something should behave.

For example, you could create a procedure (routine) that instructs the Excel application to add a new workbook to its workbook collection or add a new worksheet to an existing workbook in the worksheet collection.

[Collections are written in the plural. Thus, the Workbooks collection represents a collection of Workbook objects. By analogy, the Worksheets collection represents a collection of Worksheet objects.]

The following code snippet instructs Excel to add a new worksheet to the active workbook:

```
Sub AddWorksheet()
    Application.ActiveWorkbook.Sheets.Add Before:=Worksheets(1)
End Sub
```

`Add` is called a method and it will always be a verb. In the preceding instruction, the method can take arguments that determine how the instruction should take place. In this case, the new worksheet should be added before the first worksheet in the workbook.

If for any reason you need to abandon the instruction, you can use the `Exit Sub` statement:

```
Sub AddWorksheet()
    Exit Sub
    Application.ActiveWorkbook.Sheets.Add Before:=Worksheets(1)
End Sub
```

In the preceding example, the subroutine is exited before any worksheet is added to the workbook. Notice that here the worksheet index `1` was explicitly defined in the code. However, it is never a good idea to hardcode things into your procedures.

A better option is to pass such values as arguments of the procedure. Arguments can be optional or not. So, let us adapt the previous example so that we have two scenarios:

+ A required argument
+ An optional argument

The following screenshot shows what goes on in the code window:

```
Sub CallAddWorksheet()
    Call AddWorksheet(1
End Sub      AddWorksheet(ByVal SheetIndex As Integer)

Sub AddWorksheet(ByVal SheetIndex As Integer)
    Application.ActiveWorkbook.Sheets.Add _
        Before:=Worksheets(SheetIndex)
End Sub
```

The original subroutine now has an argument called `SheetIndex` whose value must be an integer. If the argument is anything other than an integer or is missing, VBA will throw an error. The argument of our procedure is then used as argument of the Worksheets collection.

We also need a secondary procedure from where we call the main procedure.

In order to avoid an error, we can make the argument optional. This is done as follows:

```
Sub CallAddWorksheet()
    Call AddWorksheet
End Sub

Sub AddWorksheet(Optional SheetIndex As Variant)
    If IsMissing(SheetIndex) Then SheetIndex = 1
    Application.ActiveWorkbook.Sheets.Add _
        Before:=Worksheets(SheetIndex)
End Sub
```

The first thing you will notice is that the `Integer` data type is not used. Instead, `Variant` was. The reason for this is that `Variant` is the only data type that can be missing. If `Integer` had been used, then the first value in the series would be returned, that is, a missing argument would actually be 0 (zero).

Functions

Functions, as the name suggests, return values. This contrasts to a subroutine, which is an instruction to perform an action.

Just like a subroutine, a function is also a method and it serves to supplement any missing function in Excel. Again, just like a subroutine, it may or may not have an argument. In the case it has an argument, it can also be optional.

Consider the following example:

```
Function CountWords(ByVal Text As String) As Long
    CountWords = UBound(Split(Text, " ")) + 1
End Function
```

Similar to the procedure example, here the text separator (which is an empty space given as " ") has been hardcoded into the function. In this scenario, it may not make a difference given that we are counting words and the space will be the delimiter between words. However, you can use the same method used in the procedure to pass the delimiter as an argument.

The trick in this UDF is to use the internal function named Split to split the input text into an array of words. Then, using the UBound (upper bound) function, we count the upper limit of this array. We add one to the value returned by the function; otherwise the result will be less by one word, given the lower bound of arrays.

If your function is placed in a standard module, then it will be available in your worksheet as well. When you start typing the name of functions that start with the same letters, you will be presented with a list of options as shown in the following screenshot:

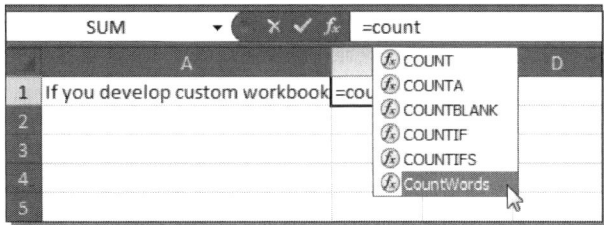

If you are not presented with the preceding screenshot, it means that **Formula AutoComplete** is not selected. In order to activate this option, you must go to **File | Excel Options | Formulas**. Then, under the **Working with formulas** group (second group from top), select the **Formula AutoComplete** option.

Functions are very versatile, which means you can use the function to calculate values in forms, worksheets, or call them from another procedure within the VBA project. Furthermore, you also call the function from another function whose final value depends on an intermediate calculation or that performed by this particular function.

In this way, you can compartmentalize the job performed by each function you create, instead of packing all calculations with a single function.

If you plan to use your custom functions in a worksheet, then the next important step is related to categorizing your function. If you open Excel's **Insert Function** dialog box (you can click on **fx** on the Formula bar or press *Alt + I + F*) you will see that all functions go into a specific category. In fact, even our custom function goes into a category (the **User Defined** category).

However, you may want to give more meaning to your function by placing it into a "proper" category.

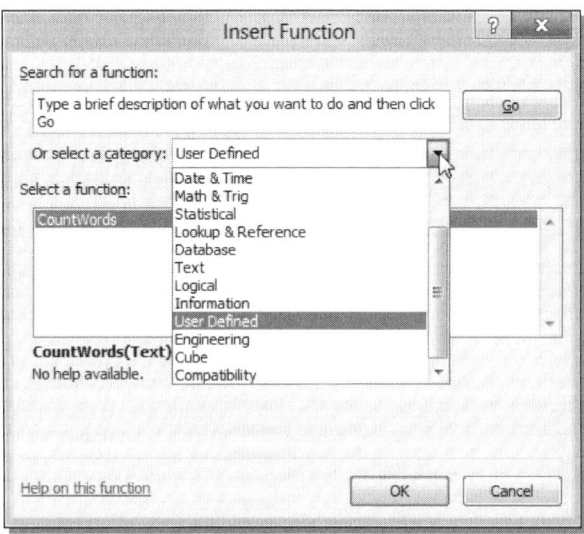

The following table shows the list of all the categories of Excel's built-in functions:

Integer value	Category name
1	Financial
2	Date & Time
3	Math & Trig
4	Statistical
5	Lookup & Reference
6	Database
7	Text
8	Logical
9	Information
10	Commands (hidden)
11	Customizing (hidden)
12	Macro (hidden)
13	DDE/External (hidden)
14	User-Defined (default for custom functions)
15	Engineering

Given that the function presented here deals with text, you may want to put it in the Text category. We will take the opportunity to add a description to it as well.

The code will run when the workbook is opened. Therefore, we will add the code to the Open event of the workbook. In order to do so, you must open the code window for **ThisWorkbook**. With the code window open, we will insert the following procedure:

```
Private Sub Workbook_Open()
    Application.MacroOptions "CountWords", _
        "This function counts the number of words in a text.", , , , , _
7
End Sub
```

After executing the preceding code, the function will be categorized as **Text** and the description will be added to it. The following screenshot shows the result:

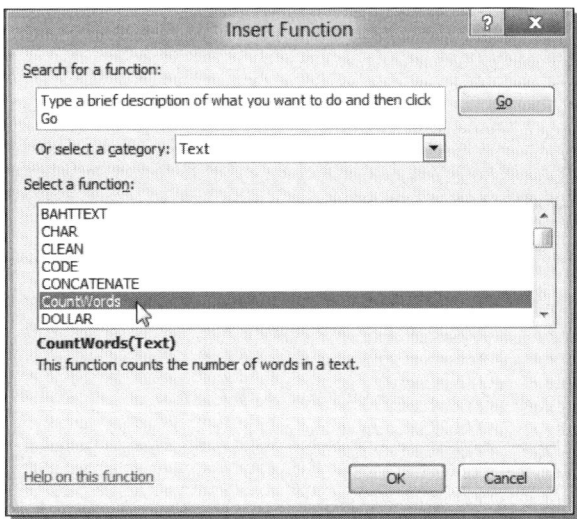

Prior to Excel 2010, we could not add description to the arguments of our functions. This has changed, which makes UDFs look much more professional than before.

Basically, we will use the same code as before, but we will add a list of arguments and the respective descriptions. It is done as follows:

```
Private Sub Workbook_Open()
'   Declare a string array with two positions
    Dim CountWordsArgs(1 To 2)            As String

'   Define the value for each position within the array
```

```
            CountWordsArgs(1) = "Type in or select the text containing " & _
                "the words you want to count..."
            CountWordsArgs(2) = "Type in the delimiter used to separate " & _
                "and count the words..."

        '   Set the MacroOptions value
            Application.MacroOptions _
                macro:="CountWords", _
                Description:="This function counts the number of " & _
                    "words in a text.", _
                Category:=7, _
                ArgumentDescriptions:=CountWordsArgs

        End Sub
```

The following screenshot shows the **Function Arguments** dialog box with the respective arguments and their descriptions:

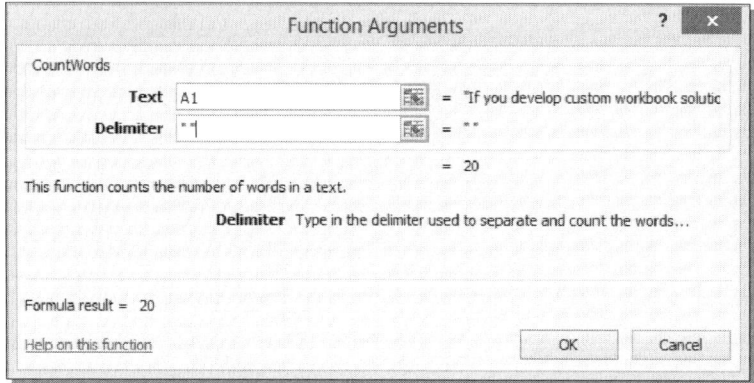

Now, let us suppose you want to have your own category, that is, instead of using any of the built-in function categories (including the **User Defined** category), you wish to have something like "PACKT Functions".

The following screenshot shows exactly this scenario. This is a great way to take your personalization to the next level.

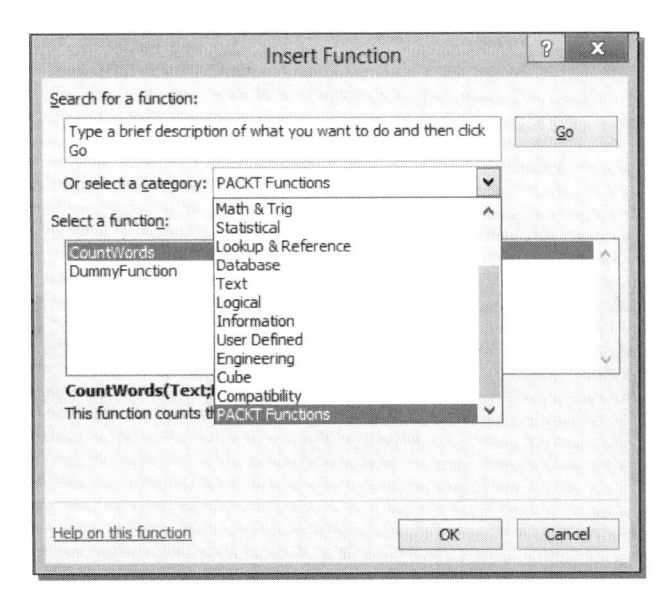

This is done as follows:

1. Right-click on any sheet and then click on **Insert…**.
2. On the dialog box that opens, select **MS Excel 4.0 Macro**.
3. Next, activate the **Formulas** tab and the click on **Define Name**.
4. In the **New Name** dialog box, enter a name for your first function. In this case, I will name `DummyFunction`.
5. Now, select **Function** from the **Macro** group. In the category drop-down list, enter whatever name you've decided to give to your custom category (here, I chose `PACKT` as the prefix, but it could be your company name, for example).

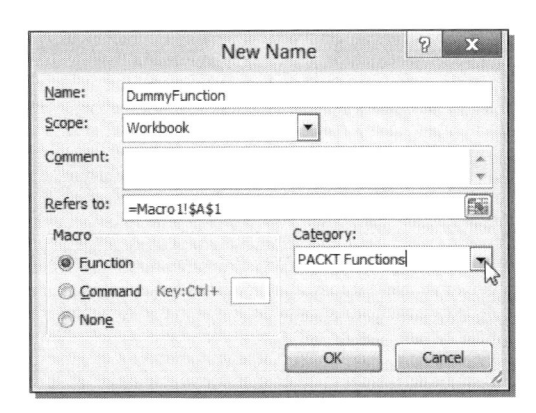

That's it, you are done. In order for you to add your custom functions to this new category, you will need to know which index represents it. Given the built-in categories, this number should start at 16. So, you should try indexes starting at 16.

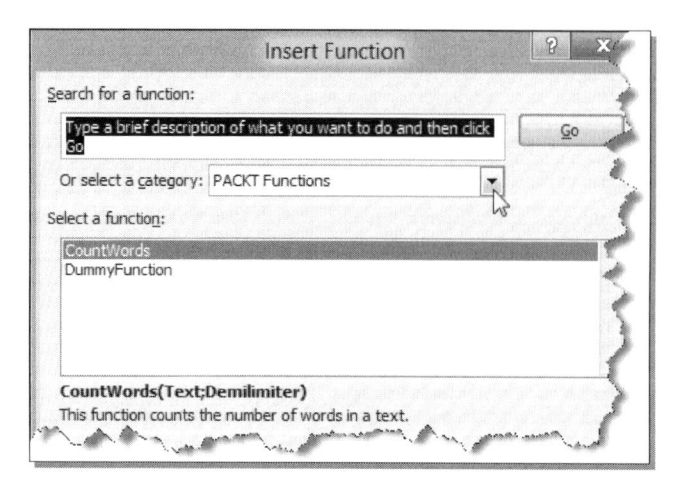

In this section, you have learned some more advanced programming techniques in VBA. You started with looping techniques where you learned different ways to loop through different types of variables such as numeric variables and objects. You also learned the importance of clearing objects from memory in order to avoid the unnecessary allocation of memory to objects which no longer need such resources. Finally, you learned how to create user-defined functions and how to set their attributes. In the next section, you will learn more specialized features such as enumeration and classes.

Top features you'll want to know about

In this section, you will learn about some VBA programming features that you will certainly want to know about. Here, you will learn how to work with enumeration, classes, and external libraries.

We will kick off by looking at enumeration.

Enumeration

The first question that might pop into your mind is, "What the heck is enumeration?" As the name suggests, it enumerates something, but what? As a rule of thumb, enumeration is a group of constants. So, supposing you have an object, it is likely that this object has a color property. Therefore, you could have a "Color" group. Then you could enumerate the colors you want to use in your code. This will make life easier when determining which color to use, given that you simply declare the enumerator and choose one of its values when the times comes.

Take a look at the following screenshot:

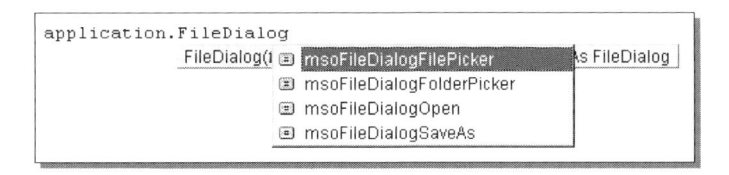

Here, we have a `FileDialog` property (which is a member of the `Application` class) that takes `FileDialogType` as an argument, which is in turn enumerated by `msoFileDialogType`. Therefore, when you try to enter an argument for this property, you are only allowed to choose from those types which have been enumerated, that is, the options that belong to the group of file dialog types.

This is a great way to reduce your workload when you need to use certain types of constants, given that you can use enumeration across your entire VBA project. Furthermore, if you make a mistake in the value of such constants, you do not need to run through your code in order to change the variable wherever it had been used. Instead, you simply change the enumeration value.

Enumerations, such as procedures and functions, can be declared as `Public` or `Private`. The scope will depend on its intended use. If you plan to use it across your VBA project, ensure you place it in a standard module.

An enumeration is declared as follows:

```
Public | Private Enum MyEnumerationName
  [Constants]
End Enum
```

Now, let us suppose we want to enumerate some colors to be used in our code, an example could be as follows:

```
Public Enum MyColors
    COLOR_BLACK = 0
    COLOR_BLUE = 12611584
    COLOR_GREEN = 5287936
    COLOR_ORANGE = 49407
    COLOR_RED = 255
    COLOR_YELLOW = 65535
End Enum
```

> If you need the value for other colors (or any other constant for that matter), simply record a macro painting the background of a cell, object, and so on. Then, inspect your code and copy the parameters from there.

The next step, of course, is to put it to good use. A screenshot of the code, when calling a subroutine that takes the custom enumeration as argument, is as follows:

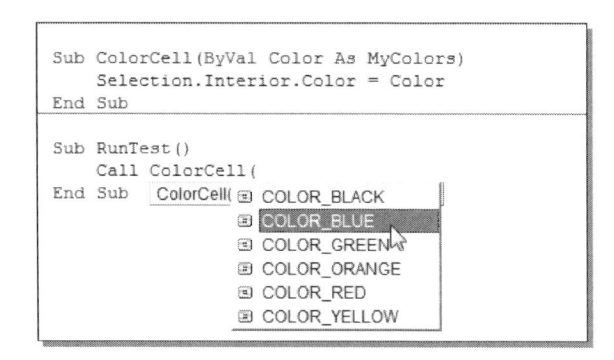

```
Sub ColorCell(ByVal Color As MyColors)
    Selection.Interior.Color = Color
End Sub

Sub RunTest()
    Call ColorCell(
End Sub    ColorCell( ⊞ COLOR_BLACK
                     ⊞ COLOR_BLUE
                     ⊞ COLOR_GREEN
                     ⊞ COLOR_ORANGE
                     ⊞ COLOR_RED
                     ⊞ COLOR_YELLOW
```

The preceding code is shown as a screenshot so that you can have a clearer idea of what happens when you call the enumeration. As explained before, you can pass a parameter to a procedure and you can also declare its type. In this example we do just that. We declare a parameter called `Color` that is declared as the `MyColors` enumeration.

When we call the procedure, we are forced to enter such a parameter and we are only given the options declared in our enumeration.

Classes

You will now learn a bit about classes. When we program, we are continuously manipulating objects. You have seen this already in this book and it is now time to create your own objects.

Bear in mind that VBA is not a truly object-oriented programming language. However, it gives us a whole lot of possibilities in terms of programming, as we can compartmentalize many tasks by encapsulating the code into such classes. We can then call such encapsulated code when necessary.

VBA provides you with icons that visually identify the types you use. The following screenshot shows a **Worksheet** object type:

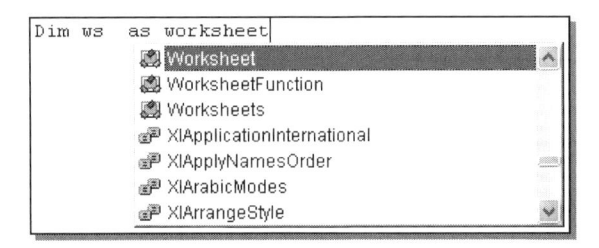

An object can be easily recognized by its icon. As mentioned at the beginning of this book, objects have properties and methods, which in turn are represented by their own set of icons.

When we explicitly dimension an object, all of its methods and properties are exposed. We get to them by adding a dot after the object's name. This is demonstrated in the following screenshot:

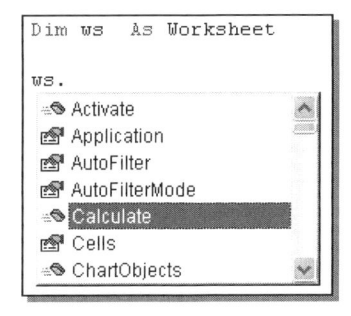

A class is simply an abstraction, but what is an abstraction? Abstraction is something that is outside of the concrete realm. In other words, an abstraction is something that has a high level of generalization.

If this sounds strange, picture a tree in your mind. What do you see? A tree is an object with a high level of generalization (abstraction) because we cannot determine what kind of tree it is until we specify its properties such as name, type, and order.

In fact, although most people would think of a tree as a woody plant, the oil industry has something called "Christmas tree", which is neither an artificial Christmas tree that we put up for Christmas nor a woody plant.

A graphical representation of this idea is shown in the following diagram:

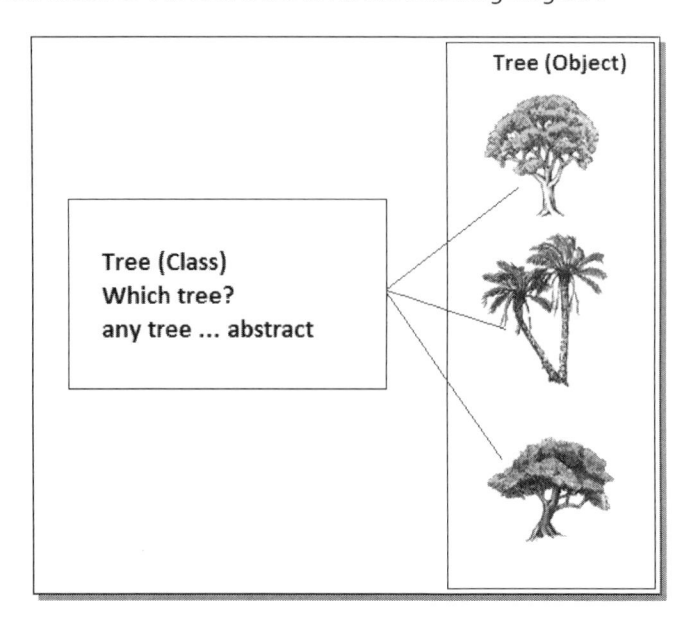

So, this is what a class is – a highly generalized object.

Another aspect of classes is that you can group such objects into collections. Collections will always be defined as plurals of such objects. So, taking the tree object as an example, we can build collections of the same type, as shown in the following diagram:

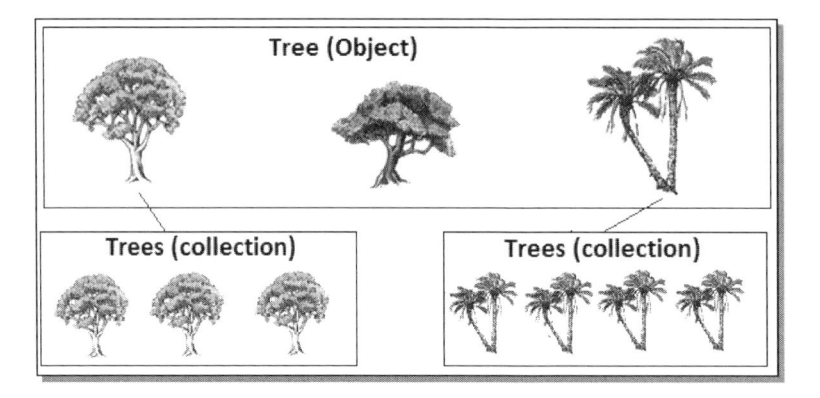

To begin with, we will insert a new class module. In order to do so, open the Visual Basic Editor (VBE) by pressing *Alt + F11* simultaneously. Then, go to **Insert | Class Module**.

Once you have inserted the class module, rename it to `clsHouse`, as shown in the following screenshot:

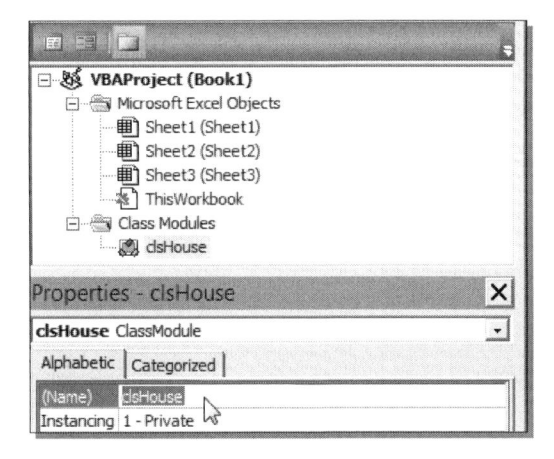

The prefix **cls** indicates that this is a class module. We will call it this way so that we can pretend that this is a generalization of a house, that is, this "house" could be a shack or a mansion for all we care.

We will now code this object and give it some properties and methods. Keep in mind the nomenclature, as for properties we use nouns and for methods we use verbs.

Here is a quick example with explanations:

```
Dim sHouseAddress As String

'The keyword "Let" of a property permits us to
'set a value for a property (write to the property)
' Here, the property is called "Address" which
'allows us to give an address to the house.
Property Let Address(ByVal HouseAddress As String)
    sHouseAddress = HouseAddress
End Property

'The keyword "Get" allows us to retrieve the
'value written to the property
Property Get Address()
    Address = sHouseAddress
End Property
```

In this class, we have one property called `Address`. This is a read-write property, as we can read from and write to it. The keyword that allows us to write to a property is `Let`. Conversely, to read a property we use the `Get` keyword.

Excel Programming with VBA Starter

The next step is to instantiate the object so that we can use it. In order to carry this out, we must add a standard module. Once this is done, we will add the following code (shown as a screenshot so that you get a better idea of what to expect):

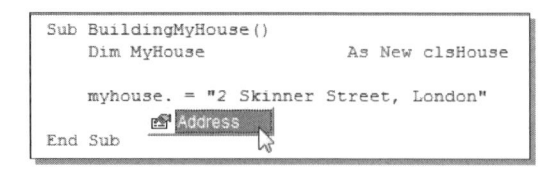

```
Sub BuildingMyHouse()
    Dim MyHouse              As New clsHouse

    myhouse. = "2 Skinner Street, London"
            Address
End Sub
```

Notice that the `MyHouse` object is dimensioned as a new instance of `clsHouse`. For now, it only has one property (`Address`) and its value will be `2 Skinner Street, London`.

Once you set the address value, you can retrieve it and show it in a message box, as follows:

```
Sub BuildingMyHouse()
    Dim MyHouse              As New clsHouse

    MyHouse.Address = "2 Skinner Street, London"
    MsgBox "My house is located at : " & MyHouse.Address
    Set MyHouse = Nothing

End Sub
```

Now, let us suppose we want to retrieve the size of this particular house. Let us further suppose that this is a fixed size, that is, we cannot change (write) this value; we can only retrieve (read) it.

We can add the following property to our class. This property is read-only, as its value is hardcoded as `"112 square meters"`:

```
Property Get Size() As String
    Size = "112 square meters"
End Property
```

We can readapt our standard module code so it would look as follows. Notice that this time the message to be shown also contains the size of the house:

```
Sub BuildingMyHouse()
    Dim MyHouse              As New clsHouse
    Dim sMsg                 As String

    MyHouse.Address = "2 Skinner Street, London"
    sMsg = "My house is located at : " & MyHouse.Address & vbCr
    sMsg = sMsg & "Its size is : " & MyHouse.Size
    MsgBox sMsg

    Set MyHouse = Nothing

End Sub
```

Once it is executed, you will get the following message box, which contains both the house's address as well as its size in square meters:

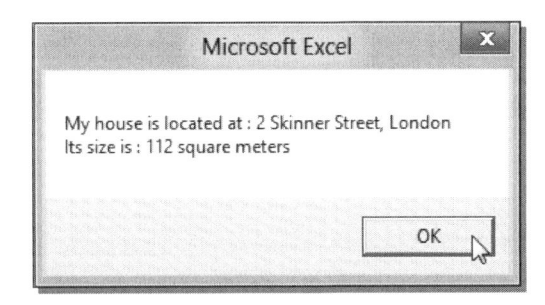

> Microsoft Excel
>
> My house is located at : 2 Skinner Street, London
> Its size is : 112 square meters
>
> OK

Although the property Size, just specified is read-only, we can create a method that instructs this size to grow. Of course, this requires a redefinition of our code.

We will make the assumption that the fixed size for any house we build is always 112 square meters. We can later add extensions to the house (make the house "grow") and that the growth (extension) must be an integer representing 1 meter at a time. So, if we instruct the size to grow (extend the size of the house) by 2, it means the size will be 2 square meters larger than the default size.

The new code in the class module could look as follows:

```vba
' Sets a global constant whose default value is 112
Const DefaultSize As Integer = 112

' Global variable to hold the address defined by the user
Dim sHouseAddress             As String

'Global variable to hold the variable containing
'the size by which the house should grow
Dim iHouseNewSize             As Integer

'Method that instructs the house to "grow"
'It takes an argument called "Meters" which is an integer
Sub Grow(ByVal Meters As Integer)
'    This integer (Meters) is added to the default size
'    of the house. The global house size (iHouseNewSize) is
'    then set.
    iHouseNewSize = DefaultSize + Meters
End Sub

'Property to return the house size
Property Get Size() As String
'    If the new size of the house is zero (the default
'    value of an integer type) then, the size of the house
```

```
'      is the default value (112 square meters)
       If iHouseNewSize = 0 Then
           Size = DefaultSize & " square meters"

'      Otherwise, it should be the new value
       Else
           Size = iHouseNewSize & " square meters"
       End If
End Property
```

We then need to change the code in the standard module. Here, we will have two different moments of the code. First, it will show the default value for the house. We will then instruct it to grow by 5 square meters and show its new size:

```
Sub BuildingMyHouse()
'      Dimension the MyHouse object
       Dim MyHouse            As New clsHouse

'      String to hold the message that will be
'      displayed in the message box
       Dim sMsg               As String

'      Set the property "Address" of the MyHouse Object
       MyHouse.Address = "2 Skinner Street, London"

'      Defines the message to display the address
       sMsg = "My house is located at : " & MyHouse.Address & vbCr

'      Shows the current size of the MyHouse object
       sMsg = sMsg & "Its size is : " & MyHouse.Size

'      Display the address and current size of the MyHouse object
       MsgBox sMsg

'      Increase the MyHouse object size by 5 square meters
       MyHouse.Grow (5)

'      Set a new message with the new values
       MyHouse.Address = "2 Skinner Street, London"
       sMsg = "My house is located at : " & MyHouse.Address & vbCr
       sMsg = sMsg & "Its new size is : " & MyHouse.Size

'      Show the new values
       MsgBox sMsg

       Set MyHouse = Nothing

End Sub
```

Another good use for classes is encapsulation. Basically, what it means is to envelope complex code in a class module and then to expose only the easy part, either through a method or a property. Think of encapsulating and putting that awful-tasting medicine in a capsule with a mint taste. The awful medicine (the code) stays inside the capsule (class module), but you only see and taste what is outside, yet it works wonders all the same.

The next example will return the name of the user currently logged in the machine. In order to do this, we will need to use a Windows API. There is a little application called **API Viewer** (refer to the *Resources* section to find out where you can download this viewer from). API Viewer exposes Windows APIs, which you can copy and paste into your project.

For this particular example, we will use the `GetUserName` API. So, to begin we will add a new class module, but this time we will name it `clsComputer`, given that we will work with functions that work together with the operating system.

Here is the API you must add to the top-most part of your class module. There is not much to say about the API, so the explanation will be added to the code we will write on top of it:

```
Private Declare Function GetUserName Lib "advapi32.dll" _
    Alias "GetUserNameA" ( _
    ByVal lpBuffer As String, _
    ByRef nSize As Long) As Long
```

[This examples assumes a 32-bit version of the API being used.]

The next job is to create a method (in this case, it will be a function) that will translate the API into a value returned by our custom function. (The method that will return the username. We will declare it as `Private`, so that it is not visible outside the class module):

```
'This is a private function to return the username
'This function is a method that belongs to this
'class module and will be user with a read-only property
Private Function ShowUserName() As String
    '   This string will work as a buffer for the username
    Dim UserName    As String

    '   Number of characters where the value returned
    '   within the buffer will be cut off. This is done
    '   using the Mid() function below
    Dim N           As Integer

    '   Sets the value of the username variable as a
    '   string containing 255 blank characters
    Username = String(255, " ")
```

```
    '   The string (buffer) "UserNamer" gets the characters
    '   refering to the user's name up to 255 characters
    '   which is being passed by the GetUserName API function
        GetUserName Username, 255

    '   Returns the position value of the first non-blank
    '   character within the string UserName
        N = InStr(1, Username, Chr(0)) - 1

        ShowUserName = Mid(Username, 1, N)
    End Function
```

With the method ready, the next step is to code the property. Basically, the `UserName` property gets its value from the preceding `ShowUserName` function:

```
Property Get Username() As String
    Username = ShowUserName()
End Property
```

Finally, in a standard module, we will insert the code that will access this property and return the currently logged-in user:

```
Sub ThisComputerSub()
    Dim ThisComputer        As New clsComputer
    MsgBox ThisComputer.UserName
End Sub
```

External libraries

You have already been introduced to referencing a library. Initially, you were introduced to the Windows Script Host Model. We will now look at other possibilities when it comes to using external libraries.

> Keep in mind that if you plan to have your VBA project used by others, then their machines must have such libraries registered too. Otherwise, your code will fail.

In the examples that will follow, you will learn how to integrate your Excel VBA project with Outlook. Let us start by adding the reference to the Outlook object model:

1. Open the Visual Basic Editor (VBE) window (press *Alt* + *F11*).
2. Go to **Tools | References**.
3. Once the dialog box is open, scroll down until you find the **Microsoft Outlook 14.0 Object Library**. Once you find it, select it and close the dialog box.

> The version referenced here is for Office 14 (Office 2010). If you open such a project in an earlier version, say, Office 2007, then the code will fail given that we have explicitly said to use version 14. Whenever possible, use references to an earlier version.

Now, we are ready to go. Here are the exercises we will perform:

1. Create a dialog box so that we can pick one or more files to be attached to an e-mail object.
2. Code a procedure that will create an Outlook e-mail object and attach the files selected.
3. Open the e-mail in Outlook so that we can add a message to it before it is sent to its recipient.

Let us start with the definition of our File Picker dialog box, so you should start by adding a new standard module. Then, add the following code. The explanation is embedded in the code:

```
'Public variable that will hold the
'string containing the file names
Public sFileName                    As String

Sub OpenFileDialogBox()
'   Dimension of the file dialog box object
    Dim objFileDialogBox            As FileDialog

'   Dimension of the file object. It will be
'   a variant as we do not know its type
    Dim objFile                     As Variant

'   Set the file dialog box as a File Picker
    Set objFileDialogBox = Application.FileDialog( _
        msoFileDialogFilePicker)

'   Set the file name string to zero-length
    sFileName = ""

'   With the File Dialog Box we will set
'   some of its properties
    With objFileDialogBox
'       Caption of the button
        .ButtonName = "Select File"

'       Permit multiple selections or not
        .AllowMultiSelect = True
```

```
'       Title of the File Dialog Box
        .Title = "Choose the files you wish to attach to the email"

'       Initial view type
        .InitialView = msoFileDialogViewDetails

'       Initial file location. The default value will be
'       the location of this workbook.
        .InitialFileName = ThisWorkbook.Path

'       Open the file dialog box
        .Show

'       Loop through the selected files
        For Each objFile In .SelectedItems
'           Write the file path and name to the
'           file name string
            sFileName = sFileName & objFile & ";"
        Next objFile
    End With


'   Remove the last semicolon in the string
    sFileName = Mid(sFileName, 1, Len(sFileName) - 1)
End Sub
```

The preceding code does not handle the cancellation event. If the user cancels the event, an error will be thrown. As an exercise, you can cancel the dialog box and see what happens. By doing so, you expose yourself to issues that will inevitably appear as you start coding in VBA.

With the file dialog out of the way, we can now move on to the e-mail. Once again, the explanation is embedded in the code:

```
Sub SendEmailWithAttachments()
'   Dimension of the Outlook application and
'   the email object item
    Dim objAppOutlook         As New Outlook.Application
    Dim objEmail              As Outlook.MailItem

'   Dimension of the attachment counter, in case more
'   than one file is selected
    Dim iAttachmentCounter    As Integer

'   Variable to split the file attachment string
    Dim varAttachments
```

```vba
    '   Call the procedure to open the File Dialog Box
        Call OpenFileDialogBox

    '   Create the Outlook email item
        Set objEmail = objAppOutlook.CreateItem(olMailItem)

    '   With the Outlook email item
        With objEmail

    '       Split the attachment string so that we can loop
    '       through the selected items
            varAttachments = Split(sFileName, ";")

    '       Loop through the array of attachments selected
            For iAttachmentCounter = 0 To UBound(varAttachments)
    '           Add the selected file as an attachment
                .Attachments.Add varAttachments(iAttachmentCounter)
            Next iAttachmentCounter

    '       Define some properties of the Outlook email item
            .Subject = "Type your subject here..."
            .Body = "Type your message here"
            .To = "rm@msofficegurus.com.br"

    '       Display the email in Outlook
            .Display
        End With

        Set objAppOutlook = Nothing
        Set objEmail = Nothing
    End Sub
```

In this section, you learned some important aspects of VBA programming such as enumeration, classes, and external libraries. Enumeration helps you standardize data entry by collecting values that belong to a predetermined category. Classes, on the other hand, help you encapsulate code that would be difficult to handle otherwise and, by doing so, you are able to streamline your programming.

Finally, you revisited referencing external libraries and learned how to interact with Outlook. This method can be used for any other library registered in your system.

Although this book was not supposed to cover all aspects of VBA, it covered the most important aspects so that you can now start digging further in order to discover more under the surface you touched here.

People and places you should get to know

If you need help with Excel, here are some people and places which will prove invaluable.

Official sites

- **Homepage**: http://office.microsoft.com/en-us/
- **Manual and documentation**: http://office.microsoft.com/en-us/excel-help/excel-help-and-how-to-FX101814052.aspx?CTT=97
- **Blog**: http://blogs.office.com/b/microsoft-excel/

Resources

- API Viewer is an application that exposes Windows APIs, which you can use in your VBA code. You can download the application from http://www.activevb.de/rubriken/apiviewer/index-apiviewer.html.
- A list of Excel MVP's websites is found at http://www.mvps.org/links.html#Excel.

Articles and tutorials

Here is a selection of VBA code samples that will help you hone your coding skills:

- **Excel ActiveX Data Objects (ADO) coding**: http://www.excelguru.ca/list.php?category/49-Excel-ADO
- **Interact with Outlook from Excel**: http://www.msofficegurus.com/post/Creating-Outlook-2007-Rules-from-Excel-2007.aspx

Community

- **Official forums**: http://answers.microsoft.com/en-us/office/forum/excel
- **Unofficial forums**: http://www.msofficegurus.com.br/forum/indice.html and http://www.mrexcel.com

Blogs

Here's a list of blogs or sites you should have at hand:

- **Excel charting**: http://peltiertech.com/
- **Excel sundries**: http://spreadsheetpage.com/
- **Excel coding**: http://www.excelguru.ca/ and http://www.cpearson.com
- **Excel tips**: http://www.rondebruin.nl/
- **Office articles**: http://www.msofficegurus.com.br/

Twitter

Here is a list of some Twitter accounts you may want to follow:

- `https://twitter.com/#!/microsoft_excel`
- `https://twitter.com/#!/exceldashboards`
- `https://twitter.com/#!/MrExcel`
- For more Open Source information, follow Packt at `http://twitter.com/#!/packtopensource`

Index

A

Addin 3
Add method 23
API Viewer 39
Application Programming Interface (APIs) 3

B

blogs
  URLs 44
bugs 11

C

classes
  about 32-40
  graphical representation 34
Const 10

D

debugging 11
Dim 10
Do-Until loop 17-19
Do-While loop 17-19
Dynamic-link Libraries (DLLs) 3

E

early binding 20
enumeration 31, 32
Excel
  blogs 44
  twitters 45
  URLs, for Official Sites 44
  URLs, for resources 44
Excel ActiveX Data Objects (ADO) coding
  URL 44
Excel VBA Starter 1
explicit variable declaration 9
external libraries 40-42

F

FileSystemObject 20
For Each-Next Loops 15
For-Next loops 13-15
functions
  about 24, 25
  built-in functions 26-28

I

Immediate window
  about 11
  code, executing 12
  displaying 11
  problems, debugging in code 11
  procedure or function, calling 12
  uses 11
implicit declaration 9
Interact with Outlook from Excel
  URL 44

L

late binding 21
loops
  Do-Until loop 17-19
  Do-While loop 17-19
  For Each-Next Loops 15
  For-Next loops 13-15
  working with 13

M

macro
 about 4
 recording 4
 recording, from Developer tab 4-6
 recording, from status bar 4
macro-enabled workbook
 saving 7
module
 adding 8

O

Object Browser 8
Object Model (OM) 16
objects
 dimensioning 20-22
 instantiating 20-22
Official forums
 URL 44
optional argument 23

P

private variable 10
public variable 10

R

referencing 16
required argument 23
routines 23

S

SheetIndex 24
Static 10
subroutines 23, 24

T

twitters
 URLs 45

U

Unofficial forums
 URL 44
User-defined Functions (UDFs) 3

V

variables
 about 9
 working with 9
VBA
 about 1, 3
 code, executing 6, 7
 features 3
 functions 3
 Immediate window 11, 12
 macro-enabled workbook, saving 7
 module, adding 8
 objects, browsing 8, 9
 using 3
 variables, working with 9, 10
VBA programming
 about 13
 Do-Until loop 17-19
 Do-While loop 17-19
 For Each-Next loops 15
 For-Next loops 13-15
 loops, working with 13
 objects, dimensioning 20-22
 objects, instantiating 20-22
 subroutines 23
 user-defined functions 24
VBA programming features
 about 31
 classes 32-39
 enumeration 31
 external libraries 40-42
Visual Basic for Applications. *See* **VBA**

About the author

Robert Martin is an Excel MVP and Microsoft Certified Professional. With a background in finance, his career has ranged from being an IT Director of an investment bank in London to doing charity work in Africa, before moving to Brazil in 2007 and setting up an IT consultancy firm and then authoring training (audiovisual and written) material on Microsoft technologies. Currently he works in Brazil as an IT Consultant.

Robert Martin has also authored the following books:

- Excel Avançado, Digerati 2008
- RibbonX: Customizing the Office 2007 Ribbon, Wiley 2008
- Excel e VBA na Modelagem Financeira: Uma Abordagem Prática, Axcel Books 2005

I would like to thank my family who is always supportive in everything I do. I would also like to thank all those people who, directly or indirectly, made this piece of work possible.

About the reviewers

Jan Karel Pieterse is a self-employed Excel expert and Microsoft Office developer. He has been running his own company (www.jkp-ads.com) since 2003 and has been an Excel MVP since 2002. Jan Karel was revision author for the book *Excel 2007 VBA programming for Dummies*.

Peter M Taylor is a creative Software Developer with an interest in Excel VBA to make solutions for business. His career spans over a period of 16 years working on main frame systems within telecommunications. At the end of 2005 Peter was ready for a career change and new challenges, and an opportunity opened up in the Health Care industry supporting industry-related applications. In his spare time, Peter updates his blog, making creative solutions for a fictional business, at http://www.peterlearningabout.blogspot.com.au.

I would like to extend my thanks to Meeta Rajani from Packt Publishing for inviting me to review this book, and my family, especially my wife Karen, for the time in making this book review possible.

Thank you for buying
Excel Programming with VBA Starter

About Packt Publishing

Packt, pronounced 'packed', published its first book "Mastering phpMyAdmin for Effective MySQL Management" in April 2004 and subsequently continued to specialize in publishing highly focused books on specific technologies and solutions.

Our books and publications share the experiences of your fellow IT professionals in adapting and customizing today's systems, applications, and frameworks. Our solution based books give you the knowledge and power to customize the software and technologies you're using to get the job done. Packt books are more specific and less general than the IT books you have seen in the past. Our unique business model allows us to bring you more focused information, giving you more of what you need to know, and less of what you don't.

Packt is a modern, yet unique publishing company, which focuses on producing quality, cutting-edge books for communities of developers, administrators, and newbies alike. For more information, please visit our website: www.packtpub.com.

About Packt Enterprise

In 2010, Packt launched two new brands, Packt Enterprise and Packt Open Source, in order to continue its focus on specialization. This book is part of the Packt Enterprise brand, home to books published on enterprise software – software created by major vendors, including (but not limited to) IBM, Microsoft and Oracle, often for use in other corporations. Its titles will offer information relevant to a range of users of this software, including administrators, developers, architects, and end users.

Writing for Packt

We welcome all inquiries from people who are interested in authoring. Book proposals should be sent to author@packtpub.com. If your book idea is still at an early stage and you would like to discuss it first before writing a formal book proposal, contact us; one of our commissioning editors will get in touch with you.

We're not just looking for published authors; if you have strong technical skills but no writing experience, our experienced editors can help you develop a writing career, or simply get some additional reward for your expertise.

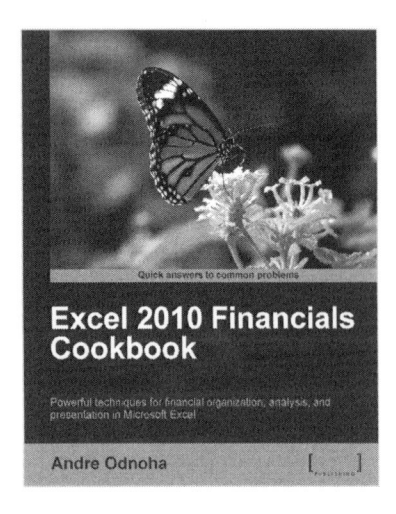

Excel 2010 Financials Cookbook

ISBN: 978-1-849691-18-5　　　Paperback: 260 pages

Powerful techniques for financial organization, analysis, and presentation in Microsoft Excel

1. Harness the power of Excel to help manage your business finances
2. Build useful financial analysis systems on top of Excel
3. Covers normalizing, analysing, and presenting financial data

VSTO 3.0 for Office 2007 Programming

ISBN: 978-1-847197-52-8　　　Paperback: 260 pages

Get to Grips with Programming Office 2007 using Visual Studio Tools for Office

1. A step-by-step guide for brand-new Office developers who want to explore programming with VSTO
2. Precise information on programming in Microsoft InfoPath, Word, Excel, PowerPoint, Outlook, Visio, and Project 2007 using VSTO
3. Create your own fully featured Office extensions

Please check **www.PacktPub.com** for information on our titles

Printed in Great Britain
by Amazon.co.uk, Ltd.,
Marston Gate.